Password K...

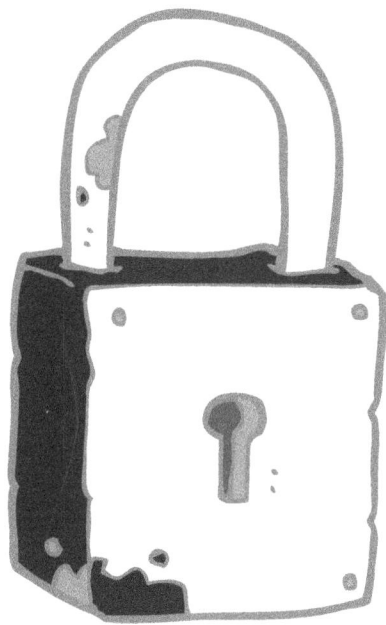

****

This logbook belongs to:

....

EightIdd Ge.Press
© Copyright 2019 - All rights reserved.
You may not reproduce, duplicate or send the contents of this
book without direct written permission from the author.

Website:
Email used:
Username:
Password:
Notes: ....
....

Website:
Email used:
Username:
Password:
Notes: ....
....

Website:
Email used:
Username:
Password:
Notes: ....
....

Website:

Email used:

Username:

Password:

Notes:

Website:

Email used:

Username:

Password:

Notes:

Website:

Email used:

Username:

Password:

Notes:

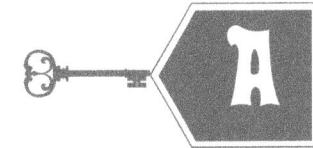

Website:
Email used:
Username:
Password:
Notes:
....
....

Website:
Email used:
Username:
Password:
Notes:
....
....

Website:
Email used:
Username:
Password:
Notes:
....
....

Website:
Email used:
Username:
Password:
Notes:

Website:
Email used:
Username:
Password:
Notes:

Website:
Email used:
Username:
Password:
Notes:

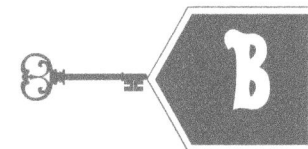

Website:
Email used:
Username:
Password:
Notes:

Website:
Email used:
Username:
Password:
Notes:

Website:
Email used:
Username:
Password:
Notes:

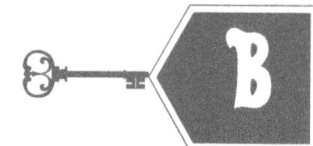

Website:
Email used:
Username:
Password:
Notes:
....
....

Website:
Email used:
Username:
Password:
Notes:
....
....

Website:
Email used:
Username:
Password:
Notes:
....
....

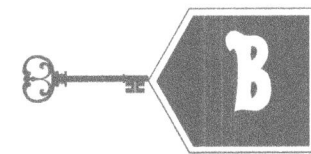

Website:
Email used:
Username:
Password:
Notes:
....
....

Website:
Email used:
Username:
Password:
Notes:
....
....

Website:
Email used:
Username:
Password:
Notes:
....
....

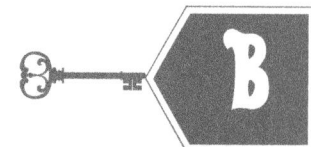

Website:
Email used:
Username:
Password:
Notes:
....
....

Website:
Email used:
Username:
Password:
Notes:
....
....

Website:
Email used:
Username:
Password:
Notes:
....
....

Website:

Email used:

Username:

Password:

Notes: ....

....

Website:

Email used:

Username:

Password:

Notes: ....

....

Website:

Email used:

Username:

Password:

Notes: ....

....

Website:
Email used:
Username:
Password:
Notes:

Website:
Email used:
Username:
Password:
Notes:

Website:
Email used:
Username:
Password:
Notes:

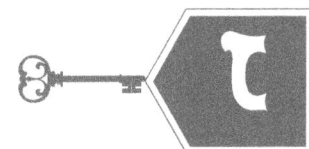

Website:
Email used:
Username:
Password:
Notes:
....
....

Website:
Email used:
Username:
Password:
Notes:
....
....

Website:
Email used:
Username:
Password:
Notes:
....
....

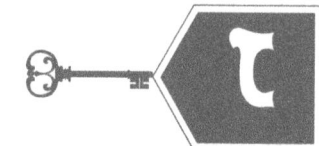

Website:

Email used:

Username:

Password:

Notes:

· ·

— · ◆ ◈ ◆ · —

Website:

Email used:

Username:

Password:

Notes:

· ·

— · ◆ ◈ ◆ · —

Website:

Email used:

Username:

Password:

Notes:

· ·

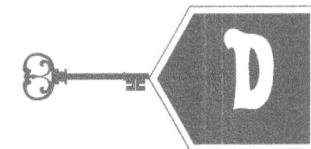

Website:
Email used:
Username:
Password:
Notes:
....
....

Website:
Email used:
Username:
Password:
Notes:
....
....

Website:
Email used:
Username:
Password:
Notes:
....
....

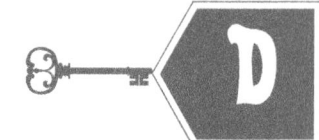

Website:
Email used:
Username:
Password:
Notes:
....

....

Website:
Email used:
Username:
Password:
Notes:
....

....

Website:
Email used:
Username:
Password:
Notes:
....

....

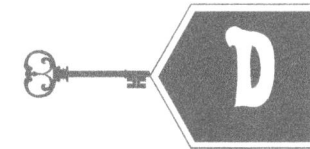

Website:
Email used:
Username:
Password:
Notes:
....
....

Website:
Email used:
Username:
Password:
Notes:
....
....

Website:
Email used:
Username:
Password:
Notes:
....
....

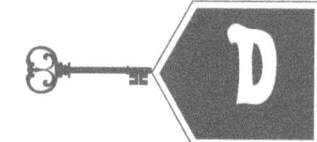

Website:
Email used:
Username:
Password:
Notes:

Website:
Email used:
Username:
Password:
Notes:

Website:
Email used:
Username:
Password:
Notes:

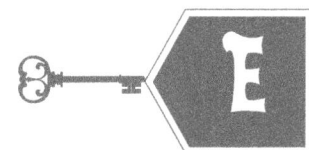

Website:
Email used:
Username:
Password:
Notes:
....

Website:
Email used:
Username:
Password:
Notes:
....

Website:
Email used:
Username:
Password:
Notes:
....

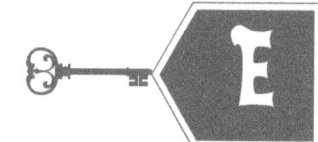

Website:
Email used:
Username:
Password:
Notes:
....

Website:
Email used:
Username:
Password:
Notes:
....

Website:
Email used:
Username:
Password:
Notes:
....

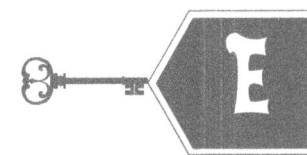

Website:
Email used:
Username:
Password:
Notes:

Website:
Email used:
Username:
Password:
Notes:

Website:
Email used:
Username:
Password:
Notes:

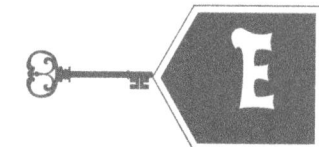

Website:
Email used:
Username:
Password:
Notes:
....
....

Website:
Email used:
Username:
Password:
Notes:
....
....

Website:
Email used:
Username:
Password:
Notes:
....
....

Website:
Email used:
Username:
Password:
Notes: ....
....

Website:
Email used:
Username:
Password:
Notes: ....
....

Website:
Email used:
Username:
Password:
Notes: ....
....

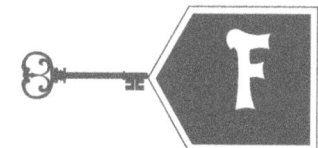

Website:
Email used:
Username:
Password:
Notes:
···
···

Website:
Email used:
Username:
Password:
Notes:
···
···

Website:
Email used:
Username:
Password:
Notes:
···
···

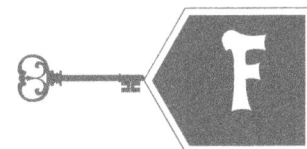

Website:
Email used:
Username:
Password:
Notes:
....

Website:
Email used:
Username:
Password:
Notes:
....

Website:
Email used:
Username:
Password:
Notes:
....

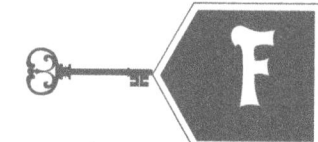

Website:
Email used:
Username:
Password:
Notes:
....

....

Website:
Email used:
Username:
Password:
Notes:
....

....

Website:
Email used:
Username:
Password:
Notes:
....

....

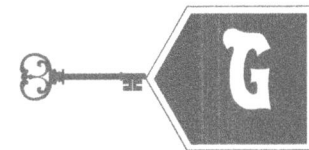

Website:
Email used:
Username:
Password:
Notes:
....

....

Website:
Email used:
Username:
Password:
Notes:
....

....

Website:
Email used:
Username:
Password:
Notes:
....

....

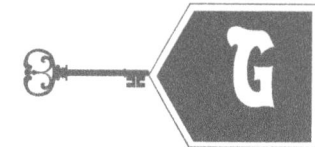

Website:

Email used:

Username:

Password:

Notes:

Website:

Email used:

Username:

Password:

Notes:

Website:

Email used:

Username:

Password:

Notes:

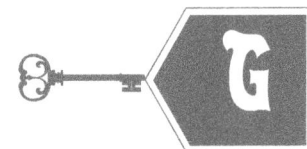

Website:
Email used:
Username:
Password:
Notes:
....
....

Website:
Email used:
Username:
Password:
Notes:
....
....

Website:
Email used:
Username:
Password:
Notes:
....
....

Website:
Email used:
Username:
Password:
Notes:

Website:
Email used:
Username:
Password:
Notes:

Website:
Email used:
Username:
Password:
Notes:

Website:
Email used:
Username:
Password:
Notes:
....
....

Website:
Email used:
Username:
Password:
Notes:
....
....

Website:
Email used:
Username:
Password:
Notes:
....
....

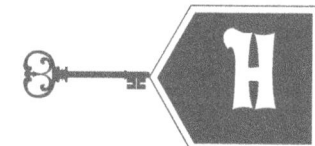

Website:
Email used:
Username:
Password:
Notes:

·····································

Website:
Email used:
Username:
Password:
Notes:

·····································

Website:
Email used:
Username:
Password:
Notes:

·····································

Website:
Email used:
Username:
Password:
Notes:
....
....

Website:
Email used:
Username:
Password:
Notes:
....
....

Website:
Email used:
Username:
Password:
Notes:
....
....

Website:
Email used:
Username:
Password:
Notes:

Website:
Email used:
Username:
Password:
Notes:

Website:
Email used:
Username:
Password:
Notes:

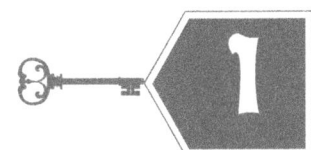

Website:
Email used:
Username:
Password:
Notes:

Website:
Email used:
Username:
Password:
Notes:

Website:
Email used:
Username:
Password:
Notes:

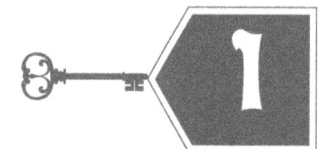

Website:

Email used:

Username:

Password:

Notes:

Website:

Email used:

Username:

Password:

Notes:

Website:

Email used:

Username:

Password:

Notes:

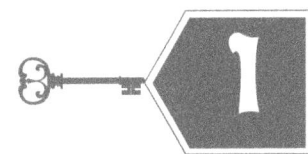

Website:
Email used:
Username:
Password:
Notes:
....

Website:
Email used:
Username:
Password:
Notes:
....

Website:
Email used:
Username:
Password:
Notes:
....

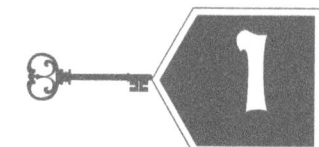

Website:
Email used:
Username:
Password:
Notes:

Website:
Email used:
Username:
Password:
Notes:

Website:
Email used:
Username:
Password:
Notes:

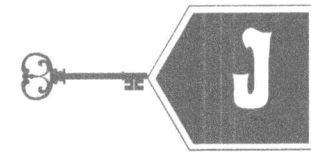

Website: _____
Email used: _____
Username: _____
Password: _____
Notes: ....
....

Website: _____
Email used: _____
Username: _____
Password: _____
Notes: ....
....

Website: _____
Email used: _____
Username: _____
Password: _____
Notes: ....
....

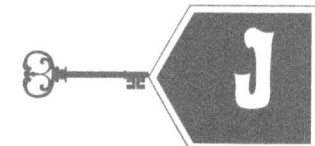

Website:
Email used:
Username:
Password:
Notes:

Website:
Email used:
Username:
Password:
Notes:

Website:
Email used:
Username:
Password:
Notes:

Website:
Email used:
Username:
Password:
Notes:
....
....

Website:
Email used:
Username:
Password:
Notes:
....
....

Website:
Email used:
Username:
Password:
Notes:
....
....

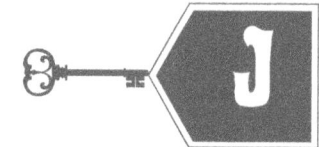

Website:
Email used:
Username:
Password:
Notes:
....

Website:
Email used:
Username:
Password:
Notes:
....

Website:
Email used:
Username:
Password:
Notes:
....

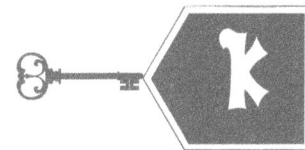

Website:
Email used:
Username:
Password:
Notes:
....
....

Website:
Email used:
Username:
Password:
Notes:
....
....

Website:
Email used:
Username:
Password:
Notes:
....
....

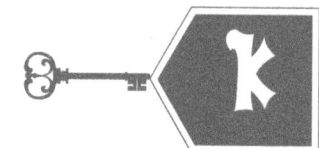

Website:
Email used:
Username:
Password:
Notes:
....
....

Website:
Email used:
Username:
Password:
Notes:
....
....

Website:
Email used:
Username:
Password:
Notes:
....
....

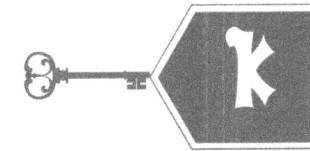

Website:
Email used:
Username:
Password:
Notes:
....
....

Website:
Email used:
Username:
Password:
Notes:
....
....

Website:
Email used:
Username:
Password:
Notes:
....
....

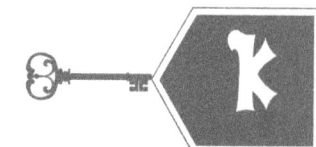

Website:
Email used:
Username:
Password:
Notes:
....
....

Website:
Email used:
Username:
Password:
Notes:
....
....

Website:
Email used:
Username:
Password:
Notes:
....
....

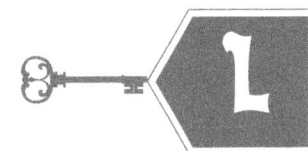

Website:
Email used:
Username:
Password:
Notes:
....
....

Website:
Email used:
Username:
Password:
Notes:
....
....

Website:
Email used:
Username:
Password:
Notes:
....
....

Website: _____
Email used: _____
Username: _____
Password: _____
Notes: _____
....
....

Website: _____
Email used: _____
Username: _____
Password: _____
Notes: _____
....
....

Website: _____
Email used: _____
Username: _____
Password: _____
Notes: _____
....
....

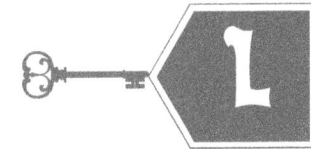

Website:
Email used:
Username:
Password:
Notes:
....
....

Website:
Email used:
Username:
Password:
Notes:
....
....

Website:
Email used:
Username:
Password:
Notes:
....
....

Website:
Email used:
Username:
Password:
Notes:
....
....

Website:
Email used:
Username:
Password:
Notes:
....
....

Website:
Email used:
Username:
Password:
Notes:
....
....

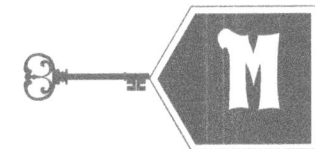

Website:
Email used:
Username:
Password:
Notes:
....
....

Website:
Email used:
Username:
Password:
Notes:
....
....

Website:
Email used:
Username:
Password:
Notes:
....
....

Website:
Email used:
Username:
Password:
Notes:
....
....

Website:
Email used:
Username:
Password:
Notes:
....
....

Website:
Email used:
Username:
Password:
Notes:
....
....

Website:
Email used:
Username:
Password:
Notes:
....
....

Website:
Email used:
Username:
Password:
Notes:
....
....

Website:
Email used:
Username:
Password:
Notes:
....
....

Website:
Email used:
Username:
Password:
Notes:

Website:
Email used:
Username:
Password:
Notes:

Website:
Email used:
Username:
Password:
Notes:

Website:
Email used:
Username:
Password:
Notes:
....
....

Website:
Email used:
Username:
Password:
Notes:
....
....

Website:
Email used:
Username:
Password:
Notes:
....
....

Website:
Email used:
Username:
Password:
Notes:
....

Website:
Email used:
Username:
Password:
Notes:
....

Website:
Email used:
Username:
Password:
Notes:
....

Website:
Email used:
Username:
Password:
Notes:

Website:
Email used:
Username:
Password:
Notes:

Website:
Email used:
Username:
Password:
Notes:

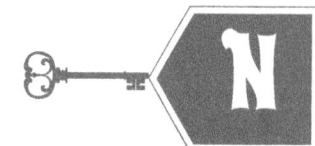

Website:

Email used:

Username:

Password:

Notes:

....

....

Website:

Email used:

Username:

Password:

Notes:

....

....

Website:

Email used:

Username:

Password:

Notes:

....

....

Website:
Email used:
Username:
Password:
Notes: ....
....

Website:
Email used:
Username:
Password:
Notes: ....
....

Website:
Email used:
Username:
Password:
Notes: ....
....

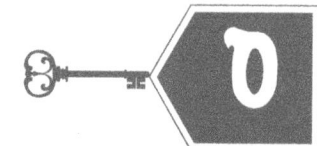

Website:
Email used:
Username:
Password:
Notes:
....

Website:
Email used:
Username:
Password:
Notes:
....

Website:
Email used:
Username:
Password:
Notes:
....

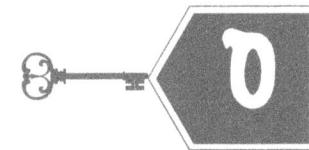

Website:
Email used:
Username:
Password:
Notes:
....

Website:
Email used:
Username:
Password:
Notes:
....

Website:
Email used:
Username:
Password:
Notes:
....

Website:
Email used:
Username:
Password:
Notes:
....
....

Website:
Email used:
Username:
Password:
Notes:
....
....

Website:
Email used:
Username:
Password:
Notes:
....
....

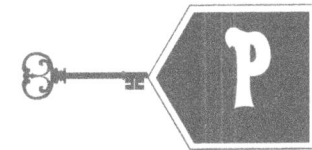

Website:
Email used:
Username:
Password:
Notes:
....
....

Website:
Email used:
Username:
Password:
Notes:
....
....

Website:
Email used:
Username:
Password:
Notes:
....
....

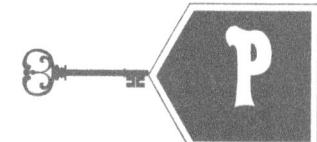

Website:
Email used:
Username:
Password:
Notes:

Website:
Email used:
Username:
Password:
Notes:

Website:
Email used:
Username:
Password:
Notes:

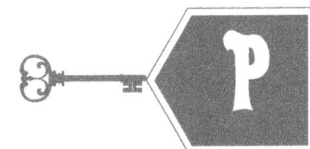

Website:
Email used:
Username:
Password:
Notes:

Website:
Email used:
Username:
Password:
Notes:

Website:
Email used:
Username:
Password:
Notes:

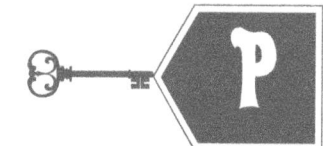

Website:
Email used:
Username:
Password:
Notes:
....

....

Website:
Email used:
Username:
Password:
Notes:
....

....

Website:
Email used:
Username:
Password:
Notes:
....

....

Website:

Email used:

Username:

Password:

Notes:

Website:

Email used:

Username:

Password:

Notes:

Website:

Email used:

Username:

Password:

Notes:

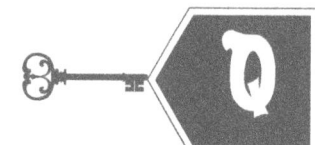

Website:
Email used:
Username:
Password:
Notes:
⋯⋯

Website:
Email used:
Username:
Password:
Notes:
⋯⋯

Website:
Email used:
Username:
Password:
Notes:
⋯⋯

Website:
Email used:
Username:
Password:
Notes:
....
....

Website:
Email used:
Username:
Password:
Notes:
....
....

Website:
Email used:
Username:
Password:
Notes:
....
....

Website:
Email used:
Username:
Password:
Notes:

Website:
Email used:
Username:
Password:
Notes:

Website:
Email used:
Username:
Password:
Notes:

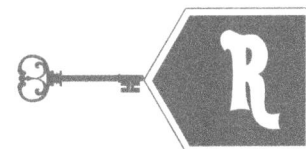

Website:
Email used:
Username:
Password:
Notes:

Website:
Email used:
Username:
Password:
Notes:

Website:
Email used:
Username:
Password:
Notes:

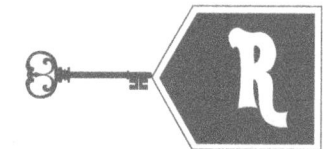

Website:

Email used:

Username:

Password:

Notes:

Website:

Email used:

Username:

Password:

Notes:

Website:

Email used:

Username:

Password:

Notes:

Website:
Email used:
Username:
Password:
Notes:
....

....

Website:
Email used:
Username:
Password:
Notes:
....

....

Website:
Email used:
Username:
Password:
Notes:
....

....

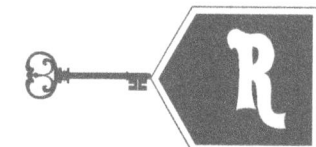

Website:
Email used:
Username:
Password:
Notes:
....
....

Website:
Email used:
Username:
Password:
Notes:
....
....

Website:
Email used:
Username:
Password:
Notes:
....
....

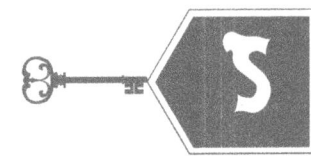

Website:
Email used:
Username:
Password:
Notes:
....
....

Website:
Email used:
Username:
Password:
Notes:
....
....

Website:
Email used:
Username:
Password:
Notes:
....
....

Website:
Email used:
Username:
Password:
Notes:
....
....

Website:
Email used:
Username:
Password:
Notes:
....
....

Website:
Email used:
Username:
Password:
Notes:
....
....

Website:
Email used:
Username:
Password:
Notes:
....
....

Website:
Email used:
Username:
Password:
Notes:
....
....

Website:
Email used:
Username:
Password:
Notes:
....
....

Website:
Email used:
Username:
Password:
Notes:
....
....

Website:
Email used:
Username:
Password:
Notes:
....
....

Website:
Email used:
Username:
Password:
Notes:
....
....

Website:
Email used:
Username:
Password:
Notes:
....
....

Website:
Email used:
Username:
Password:
Notes:
....
....

Website:
Email used:
Username:
Password:
Notes:
....
....

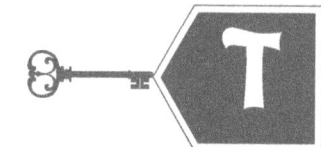

Website:
Email used:
Username:
Password:
Notes:
....

Website:
Email used:
Username:
Password:
Notes:
....

Website:
Email used:
Username:
Password:
Notes:
....

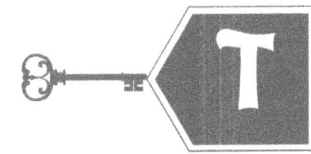

Website:
Email used:
Username:
Password:
Notes: ....
....

Website:
Email used:
Username:
Password:
Notes: ....
....

Website:
Email used:
Username:
Password:
Notes: ....
....

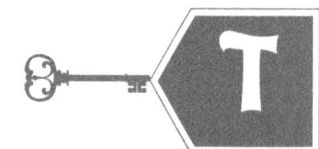

Website:
Email used:
Username:
Password:
Notes:
....

....

Website:
Email used:
Username:
Password:
Notes:
....

....

Website:
Email used:
Username:
Password:
Notes:
....

....

Website:
Email used:
Username:
Password:
Notes:

Website:
Email used:
Username:
Password:
Notes:

Website:
Email used:
Username:
Password:
Notes:

Website:
Email used:
Username:
Password:
Notes:

Website:
Email used:
Username:
Password:
Notes:

Website:
Email used:
Username:
Password:
Notes:

Website:
Email used:
Username:
Password:
Notes:

Website:
Email used:
Username:
Password:
Notes:

Website:
Email used:
Username:
Password:
Notes:

Website:
Email used:
Username:
Password:
Notes:
....
....

Website:
Email used:
Username:
Password:
Notes:
....
....

Website:
Email used:
Username:
Password:
Notes:
....
....

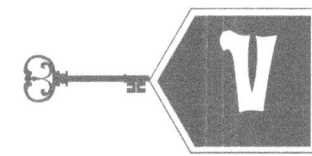

Website:
Email used:
Username:
Password:
Notes:
....
....

Website:
Email used:
Username:
Password:
Notes:
....
....

Website:
Email used:
Username:
Password:
Notes:
....
....

Website:
Email used:
Username:
Password:
Notes:
....

Website:
Email used:
Username:
Password:
Notes:
....

Website:
Email used:
Username:
Password:
Notes:
....

Website:
Email used:
Username:
Password:
Notes:
....

Website:
Email used:
Username:
Password:
Notes:
....

Website:
Email used:
Username:
Password:
Notes:
....

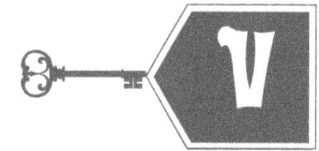

Website:
Email used:
Username:
Password:
Notes:

Website:
Email used:
Username:
Password:
Notes:

Website:
Email used:
Username:
Password:
Notes:

Website:
Email used:
Username:
Password:
Notes:
....
....

Website:
Email used:
Username:
Password:
Notes:
....
....

Website:
Email used:
Username:
Password:
Notes:
....
....

Website:
Email used:
Username:
Password:
Notes:
....

....

Website:
Email used:
Username:
Password:
Notes:
....

....

Website:
Email used:
Username:
Password:
Notes:
....

....

Website:
Email Used:
Username:
Password:
Notes:
....

Website:
Email Used:
Username:
Password:
Notes:
....

Website:
Email Used:
Username:
Password:
Notes:
....

Website:
Email used:
Username:
Password:
Notes:
....
....

Website:
Email used:
Username:
Password:
Notes:
....
....

Website:
Email used:
Username:
Password:
Notes:
....
....

Website:
Email used:
Username:
Password:
Notes:
....
....

Website:
Email used:
Username:
Password:
Notes:
....
....

Website:
Email used:
Username:
Password:
Notes:
....
....

Website:
Email used:
Username:
Password:
Notes:
··

Website:
Email used:
Username:
Password:
Notes:
··

Website:
Email used:
Username:
Password:
Notes:
··

Website:
Email used:
Username:
Password:
Notes:

Website:
Email used:
Username:
Password:
Notes:

Website:
Email used:
Username:
Password:
Notes:

Website:
Email used:
Username:
Password:
Notes:
....
....

—·◆◇◆·—

Website:
Email used:
Username:
Password:
Notes:
....
....

—·◆◇◆·—

Website:
Email used:
Username:
Password:
Notes:
....
....

Website:
Email used:
Username:
Password:
Notes:
....
....

Website:
Email used:
Username:
Password:
Notes:
....
....

Website:
Email used:
Username:
Password:
Notes:
....
....

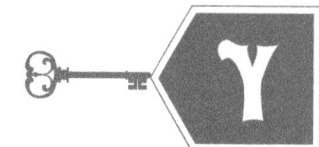

Website:
Email used:
Username:
Password:
Notes:
....

Website:
Email used:
Username:
Password:
Notes:
....

Website:
Email used:
Username:
Password:
Notes:
....

Website:
Email used:
Username:
Password:
Notes:
....
....

Website:
Email used:
Username:
Password:
Notes:
....
....

Website:
Email used:
Username:
Password:
Notes:
....
....

Website:
Email used:
Username:
Password:
Notes:
....
....

Website:
Email used:
Username:
Password:
Notes:
....
....

Website:
Email used:
Username:
Password:
Notes:
....
....

Website:
Email used:
Username:
Password:
Notes:
....
....

Website:
Email used:
Username:
Password:
Notes:
....
....

Website:
Email used:
Username:
Password:
Notes:
....
....

Z

Website:
Email used:
Username:
Password:
Notes:

Website:
Email used:
Username:
Password:
Notes:

Website:
Email used:
Username:
Password:
Notes:

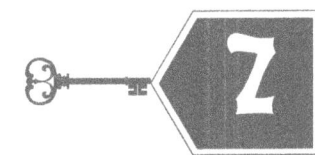

Website:
Email used:
Username:
Password:
Notes:

Website:
Email used:
Username:
Password:
Notes:

Website:
Email used:
Username:
Password:
Notes:

Website:
Email used:
Username:
Password:
Notes:
....
....

Website:
Email used:
Username:
Password:
Notes:
....
....

Website:
Email used:
Username:
Password:
Notes:
....
....

We hope
you enjoyed our book !

Our goal, as a small family company is making your experience a great one.
There's nothing better than reading the valuable feedback from you,
so please let us know if you like our book at :
eightidd@gmail.com
or leave a review with your thoughts about it.

Thanks for your amazing support !

Lightning Source UK Ltd.
Milton Keynes UK
UKHW021855161220
375343UK00008B/325